I0835361

Hymn to Sea

Art Aeon

Art Aeon/ ***Hymn to Sea***

ISBN: 9781990060342

Publisher: AEON PRESS, Halifax, Nova Scotia, Canada
E-mail: canaeonpress@gmail.com

An old version of this book was published in 2007 by AEON PRESS under the title:
Prayer to Sea by Art Aeon.

<Revised: Feb 2025>

Books of Poetry by Art Aeon

Flowing with Seasons (2003)
Hymn to Shining Mountains: The Canadian Rockies (2004)
In the Range of Light: The Yosemite (2005)
Snowflakes on Old Pines (2006)
Prayer to Sea (2007)
Echoes from Times Past (2008)
Breathing in Dao [道] (2009)
The Final Day of Socrates (2010)
Beyond the Tragedies of Oedipus and Antigone (2011)
Dù Fǔ [杜 甫] *and a Pilgrim* (2012)
The Yosemite: Images and Echoes (2013)
Revealing Dream of Vergil (2014)
Homer and Odysseus (2017)
Socrates with Xantippe on his Last Day (2019)*
Tragic Comedies of Humans (2019)*
Du Fu [杜 甫] *with his Last Pilgrim* (2019)*
Virgil's Last Dream of Aeneas and Homer (2019)*
Following Homer's Odyssey (2020)*
Human Causes of the Trojan War (2020)*
Awakening to One's Conscience (2020)*
Dante's Sublime Poem of Light (2022)*
On the Nature of Humankind (2022)*
Cosmic Drama of Nature (2022)*
Tribute to Mentors and Friends (2023)*
Pilgrimage into Classics (2024)*
Simple Songs on Life in Nature (2024)*
Inner Voice *{2000-2007}: Simple Songs on Nature*(2024)*

*Distributed worldwide by Amazon.com as printed books and by Google Play Books.com as electronic books.

Hymn to Sea

A collection of seventy short poems.
They sing of the magnificent beauty,
the profound mystery and the sublime
spirituality of the sea in simple songs.

List of Poems

List of Poems

List of Poems

List of Poems

List of Poems

For
whoever loves
the magnificent beauty
and reveres the profound mystery
and sublime spirituality
of nature

{1}

Beyond the Horizon

Sailing on the immense sea,
I gaze at the curved horizon.

How deeply it inspires my soul,
elated in awe, wonders, and thrills.

Beyond the vast mystic horizon,
I yearn to see the sublime.

{2}

Acadie (Nova Scotia)

This ethereal landmass looms
like a colossal leviathan.

It swims in the deep, boundless water
to reach its mysterious abode.

This is the blessed land of freedom,
embraced by the vast Atlantic.

May I sing of our good people,
who toil to rejoice here in peace.

{3}

Cape Breton

Here ends this continent.
The vast, fathomless sea extends.

The curved horizon hovers
over the Atlantic Ocean.

Migrating whales swim afar,
shimmering like subtle mirages.

A voyager ponders how to sail
safely across the mystic sea of being.

{4}

Seascape

The vibrant sea embraces
a cozy, sheltered cove.

Twin peaks of an islet
soar up from the deep water.

Pairs of seals play
on perpetual billows.

I gaze at the vast horizon,
breathing out infinity.

{5}

Margaree River

An old wooden bridge crosses
over gentle *Margaree River.*

It flows into the immense sea,
glittering at a serene sunset.

A graceful heron alights
on a submerged tree stump.

She poises so still, as if
painted in a mythical picture.

{6}

Prayer at Sunset

At sunset, I reach the high headland,
jutting out to the vast shining sea.

The red sun disc blazes the curved horizon.
It dips into the glittering water.

Beauteous afterglows suffuse
the pristine coasts and serene sea.

Rapt in awe, wonders, and sheer thrills,
I bow to the sublime grandeur of nature.

{7}

Strolling Carefree

Early on a pleasant, clear morning,
I stroll around a serene, cozy cove.

Playful waves sing and dance
by the pristine, vibrant seashores.
Fresh breezes gently caress me.

I gather exquisite driftwood
to build a fanciful castle on the sand.

The open sea and sky embrace my soul:
Free, happy, and thankful in peace.

Along the Cabot Trails

Steep, rocky cliffs plunge into the vast sea.
Winding roads weave in sudden turns.

The breath-taking panorama unfolds
before my awe-astounded vision.

I seem to dive deep into the sea;
Then, soar up high to reach the heavens.

{9}

Sanctuary in Cape Breton

Hiking along the coastal trails
in the Cape Breton Highlands,
I admire stark, steep, sheer cliffs,
sculpted by the incessant sea.

Rare animals freely roam
in this secluded haven:
Moose wave comely antlers;
Great herons glide in the sky.

How wondrous to breathe in
the pristine beauty of nature!
I adore this peaceful land,
singing with the vibrant sea.

{10}

Sea Sculptures

Picturesque clouds float
in the deep azure sky.

The vast blue sea embraces
rugged, pristine, stark coasts.

Lively billows hew hard rocks
into sheer wondrous sculptures
through countless cycles of seasons.

Here, one breathes in one's eternity.

{11}

A Haven by Sea

Little islets dot the immense sea
like gems sparkling on the blue water.

Green carpets of junipers adorn
pristine seacoasts, rolling in peace.

A hidden, graceful cove cuddles
playful waves lapping from the sea.

A rare seabird leaves cute footprints:
Cryptic poems written on sand.

{12}

Crescent Beach

The vibrant sea embraces
a hidden crescent sandy beach.

A flock of blue herons
reposes in timeless still.

The resplendent sun sets
on the glowing horizon.

A meek soul breathes in
the blissful sublimity in a trance.

On the Skyline Trail

The splendid sun sets on the immense sea,
pouring out its glorious golden rays.

Suddenly, gusty winds bring dark clouds.
They clash in lightning and thunder.
Thick hail and rain pour down,
drenching a hiker on a bare, stark headland.

The thunderstorm stops as quickly
as it started, a graceful rainbow bedecks
the misty, pristine coastal mountains.
The setting sun beams wondrous lights.

The calm sea gleams ablaze in afterglows.
The elated soul muses in a deep trance.

{14}

Musing on Shining Stars

Camping on the *Tancook Island,*
a tiny isle afloat on the Atlantic,
I stay awake on a tranquil night.

Countless stars look so bright and close,
as if they came down to reveal
mysteries of the expanding universe:

"Why have you been burning out
your masses in such fierce passions?

How long have you been running away
from each other so fast and afar?

Who will stay awake here, and till when,
to watch your abstruse cosmic drama?"

{15}

In Kejimkujik Park

The vast, serene lake
reflects the clear blue sky
like a huge mirror
in a wonderland.

My sleek canoe glides
on the limpid, silken water.
Adrift carefree, I dream
in this surreal, ethereal realm.

Songs of the unseen loons
echo on the pristine shores.
Blissful peace pervades
deeply into my inner lake.

{16}

A Fishing Cove

The sun sets on the serene sea,
glittering in splendours.

Unearthly peace deepens
in a calm, sheltered cove.

An old pier cuddles
a small fishing boat.

A lone egret alights on
its bare mast and rests.

{17}

Cape Split

Stark headlands split into colossal crags.
Miles of crimson clays vanish into the sea.

A stout eagle soars up along steep sheer cliffs.
Colourful flowers dance in fresh sea breezes.

Wild high tides surge into the vast, wide basin.
Whitecaps waft on turbid rushing billows.

The Bay of Fundy roars primeval calls.
Their echoes reverberate in the depths of my heart.

{18}

Abegweit (Prince Edward Island)

Amid the vast Gulf of Saint Lawrence,
a dreamy island, *Abegweit,* floats in peace.
Green meadows gently meander
to merge with crimson cray beaches.
Blue herons gently glide around shores,
caressed by lapping waves from the sea.

Alone at a small, cozy gable
of a friendly old farmhouse,
I stay awake on a still, moonlit night.

Amid the deep sounds of the vast sea,
I seem to hear the vivacious
laughter and heartfelt sobs
of our dear Anne of *Green Gable.*
Her frank, kindly spirit
and beautiful imaginations
make this remote island
a vivid, enchanting dreamland.

{19}

Peggy's Cove

An old lighthouse stands alone
on stark, rocky cliffs at *Peggy's Cove.*

It looks out the boundless sea,
keeping profound, prophetic silence
on vicissitudes of our life.

Who was Peggy? What did she do
to leave here her sweet name?
The legends of simple people
with good gentle hearts murmur
in the cryptic voice of the ageless sea.

Hiking around Peggy's Cove

We hike on stark, rugged seacoasts
around the panoramic *Peggy's Cove.*

How wondrous it is to breathe in
fresh vitality of the vast, vibrant sea!

The mystic horizon looms so closely,
as if we might peek the beyond.

We are nature's little children:
In delight, we sing of her grace.

{21}

Voice of Sea

The mystic voice of the immense sea
resounds on the pristine seashores.

What does it speak to this meek soul
in such a fathomless mystery?

Elated in deep awe and wonder,
I strive to grasp what the sea sings.

The Stormy Sea

Roaring gales gust over
wild, rugged seacoasts.

Enraged billows pound
rough, craggy, sheer cliffs.

The stark headland looks
utterly forlorn.

Yet, how much I love
this austere beauty!

{23}

Moonlit Seashores

The lucent full moon rises
above the vast horizon.
Silvery beams glitter
on the immense sea.

A fishing boat comes home
safely in limpid moonlight.
Playful waves caress
this peaceful, cozy cove.

A humble man muses
strolling along seashores.
Unearthly calm prevails
the moonlit, mystic sea.

{24}

A Pair of Seabirds

A fine, delicate lace
of fragile ice bedecks
the sheltered crescent shore
of a small hidden cove.

A pair of seabirds alights
on their cozy haven.
How peacefully they rest
in such warm, tender love!

{25}

In my Haven by Sea

The boundless sea sings
in a deep, mystic voice.
Vibrant waves caress
pristine, scenic coasts.

Refreshing sea-breezes
invigorate my heart.
The curved horizon
inspirits my vision.

Atop a steep, windy cliff,
I kneel on my blessed haven
to thank for this blissful peace
amid tense struggles in our lives.

{26}

Misty Sea

Dense mists sweep on calm shores.
The sea disappears and reappears
like vague images in a dream.

What do these subtle feelings sculpt
into the mystic recess in me?
The most profound mystery is this mind.

{27}

By the Frozen Sea

The pallid sun sets on the frozen sea
in sombre, austere, impressive grandeur.

Serene, dim dusk shrouds a lonesome figure,
kneeling humbly in earnest prayer:

"May I sail across this mystic sea of being
to reach the enlightened realm safely."

{28}

Prayer to Sea

I come to you, sea,
to confide my joys and woes,
passing through this life.

Sing to me what you
know of this mystic voyage
to find my true home.

{29}

Cosmic Music

Limpid moonlight gleams
on vibrant waves; vast sea sings
deep, cosmic music.

{30}

Double Storms

Dour squalls thrash headlands.
Seething billows beat bleak shores.

Climbing up stark cliffs,
I strive to quench fierce storms,
surging in this anguished heart.

{31}

Winter Journey

Lucent full moon shines
the calm sea. Cold austere night
deepens in stillness.

A man roams over frozen shores.
May he find a warm haven.

{32}

Winter Hike

Along ice-glazed seacoasts,
I wade through a deep sea of snow
elated in sheer thrills.
How wondrous 'tis to breathe in
the austere beauty of winter!

{33}

Sunset at Sea

The blazing sun disc touches
the curved horizon of the immense sea.
Resplendent lights imbue the sky,
the sea, and the coasts in splendour.

Soon, the sun disc dips into the sea.
The impressive afterglow of the sunset
suffuses the peaceful lands, the serene sea,
and an ethereal sea in me.

{34}

Winter's Lull

Frozen seashores doze
in a lull, hungry seagulls rest
on pale, drifting ice.

{35}

Spring Stupor

Fogs shroud the livid sea.
Chilly rainstorms drench bleak lands.
A paltry froth fleets.

{36}

In Snow

Snowflakes bloom on pines.
Seagulls rest on floating ice.
A man strolls in thoughts.

{37}

The Moon in Clouds

Through drifting dark clouds
the pale moon peeks above the sombre sea.

How I wish to purge it
from the tempestuous tumults
to shine into my heart!

{38}

Double Tempests

Tempests surge at sea.
Old piers withstand wild billows.
I bear inner storms.

{39}

Workaday

In the twilight, I walk home
on a tranquil sea of snow—
happy to rest at the warm hearth
with my beloved family in love.

{40}

Thunderstorms

Fierce thunders pierce the sky.
The seething sea strikes stark, bleak lands.
I quell dire squalls in me.

Old Sailors' Tombstones

Fading epitaphs weather out
harsh, salty billows of the vibrant sea.

They invoke stout souls lost at sea
to come alive in this timid mind.

{42}

Hiking in Mists

Around steep *Chebucto Head,*
we hike along pristine coasts.
We wade through subtle mists
arising from the hiding sea.

Listening to a deep voice
of the prophetic sea,
we muse on the things past
and our dreams to fulfil.

{43}

Planting Pine Seedlings

On our pristine land, caressed by sea waves,
we toil to plant tender, little pine seedlings.

We strive to clear wild bushes and weeds.
We struggle to till hard, stubborn soils.

Fresh sea breezes clean our sweat,
and invigorate our thankful hearts.

We finish our work at sunset.
The sun disc dips into the sea.

We pray, elated in awe and thrill:
"May the seedlings grow to form pine groves."

{44}

Bay of Hope

How wondrous to come back
to our pristine haven by the sea:
Lush groves of pine trees greet us
along the pleasant, vibrant seashores.

We camp beneath the green canopy of pines:
We relish delicious foods cooked on campfires;
We stroll along the seashores and collect shells;
We listen to the inspiring voice of the sea.

Calm dusk deepens after a glorious sunset.
Twinkling stars flow in shining rivers of light.
The vast Milky Way wheels over our heads.
Elated souls pray in awe with heartfelt thanks.

{45}

Camping at *Bay of Hope*

In the twilight of calm early dawn,
tender pines play with fresh sea breezes.

Our children are sound asleep in tents,
roving in their beautiful dreams.

Strolling along vibrant shores in peace,
I listen to the profound voice of the sea in bliss.

{46}

On Beach Meadow Beach

The vast, vibrant sea caresses
miles of a silvery, sandy beach in peace.

The boundless sky embraces
the curved horizon of the mystic sea.

Enchanted on this ethereal beach,
I wade along the gently lapping waves
rapt in a blissful trance.

{47}

Dawn of Awakening

A mysterious, pristine dawn
hovers over the serene, immense sea.

Profoundly moving, ineffable hues
imbue this unearthly moment.

Kneeling on his beloved sandy beach,
a lone soul prays for the spiritual dawn
of inner awakening to his conscience.

{48}

The Sea in Me

May I sing of the sea
deep in my soul—vast, mystic,
and ethereal sea.

{49}

A Bird and a Child

Crescent sandy beach embraces
playful waves from the vast sea.

A lone little bird leaves
fleeting footprints on the shore.

Sunset suffuses the beauteous sea.
A child in me follows the bird.

{50}

Canoeing at Sea

I paddle a tiny canoe,
gliding on the limpid sea.

Fresh, cool breezes cleanse my heart,
dancing with playful waves.

Bless this frail, fleeting froth,
adrift-free on a vibrant sea of life!

{51}

Silent Night

Serene sea reflects
shimmering stars; I listen
to cosmic silence.

{52}

A Heron at Sunset

Calm sunset suffuses
graceful sea; a lone heron
glides in afterglow.

{53}

Ecstasy

Climbing up seacoasts
I listen to Beethoven's
Choral Symphony;

Into this cosmic music,
my soul seems to sublimate.

{54}

Into Words

Teach me, timeless sea,
how to put what I imagine
into firm, plain words.

{55}

Tides in Life

Hard times in life come and go
like tides at sea surge and ebb.

Yet the sea remains the same,
holding endless changes in poise.

May my inner sea embrace
tides of emotions in peace.

{56}

Plea

Let me sing of the sea
to purge my heart from anguishes
in this journey of life.

{57}

A Froth on Sea

A fleeting froth floats
on the sea of life— may he reach
the sea deep in him.

{58}

My Sea

I long for my sea:
She knows what I feel at heart;
She sings what I yearn for.

{59}

Evening Walk

Lithe mists waft on the sea.
Fresh breezes cleanse my mind; may pure
poems bloom in it.

{60}

Repose in Sea

Magnanimous sea—
when I pass this life, let me
rest in your bosom.

{61}

Dawn at Sunset

Sunset glows on the sea.
A man prays: *"May inner dawn*
enlighten this soul."

{62}

Sea at Rest

Tranquil sea reposes
in ethereal peace. A man
breathes in eternity.

{63}

Voice in Me

Unseen sea in me—
I strive to grasp its deep voice,
tolling in silence.

{64}

To Oneself

To reach the sea in me
I write *Hymn to Sea;* may it
purge and soothe my soul.

{65}

Offering

Simple songs of love
to the sea of life—may this flow
ever from heart to heart.

{66}

Prayer

Let me find peace in the sea
when I pass through this transient life.

May my soul merge with the sea
to sing of the lofty Cosmic Spirit.

{67}

Into Ancient Myth

An old man paddles
a tiny, lone canoe,
gliding on the sea
at a calm sunset.

A noble bird hovers
over his vision,
like the sacred *Ma'at,*
guiding his soul.

The man and the bird
fade away in the twilight,
sailing to their home
in the ancient myth.

{68}

For Inner Awakening

Over this peaceful land,
caressed by the immense sea,
a cold, still winter night
deepens in surreal serenity.

Beautiful stars shine
in rivers of light,
across the infinite vault,
embracing the sea.

A new millennium dawns
in our brief history,
on this tiny planet,
fleeting in the boundless void.

On the frozen seacoast,
a humble man prays alone
for an inner awakening
into the enlightened realm.

{69}

Confession

"Why do you struggle to write
in a foreign tongue, something
which nobody would care to read?"

"I toil to sing deep from my soul
what I feel, think, imagine, and yearn for
as plain, earnest, and deep as I can
to the mystic, magnanimous sea in me."

{70}

Inner Voice

A fleeting froth floats
on the mystic sea of being.
He prays in earnest:
"May I reach the unseen sea in me
to grasp its profound, wise voice,
tolling in eloquent silence."

An inner voice resounds
deep in his humble soul:
"Here, a point merges into infinity;
Your brief life into eternity."

Epilogue

This collection of simple songs was gleaned from plain diaries of our workaday life on the pristine Atlantic coasts of Canada over a half century.

I am deeply thankful to my beloved family who has inspired me to sing of our mundane life with new meanings, zest, and devotion with heartfelt love.

Art Aeon

www.ingramcontent.com/pod-product-compliance
Lightning Source LLC
LaVergne TN
LVHW050939080826
845145LV00004B/1334

* 9 7 8 1 9 9 0 0 6 0 0 5 2 *